Good
Without You

By: Britt Wolfe

This Novella Is Dedicated to:

Those who had to raise themselves up.

This is for everyone who grew up with their bullies living under their own roof. For those who learned too soon that love and cruelty can wear the same face, that family can be both your beginning and your deepest wound.

This is for the ones who fought to be seen, to be valued, to be something more than a footnote in their own homes. For the ones who had to claw their way out of the shadows cast by people who should have protected them.

And this is for those who made it out. For the ones who chose themselves, who built lives out of the wreckage of what was denied to them. For those who know that survival is only the first step, and that healing is the defiant act of refusing to let the past define you.

I know the struggle. I know the weight of it. But I also know this—there is freedom in letting go, in stepping into a world where you are no longer asking to be loved by people incapable of loving you the way you deserve.

You are not broken. You are not unworthy. You are proof that life can be beautiful, even after everything.

This story is for you.

Good Without You
Is Inspired by: *Mean*
by Taylor Swift

Since the release of Speak Now (Taylor's Version, of course), Taylor Swift's Mean has always struck me as more than just a story of spitefulness and bullying—it's an anthem of empowerment. It's a tale of reclaiming power from someone who sought to keep it for themselves, a journey of finding freedom in the face of relentless meanness. Beneath the surface of its defiance, though, there's a profound sadness—a longing for something better that never came, and the bittersweet realization that thriving means leaving behind what no longer serves you.

In today's world, where family dynamics often carry unspoken expectations and cycles of harm are perpetuated under the guise of love, I wanted to take the emotions in Mean and plant them in a story of a father and daughter. This is a story about the ways cruelty can live within kindness, of the small wounds that fester over years, and of the hope that maybe, someday, things might be different. It's about the courage to finally say, "No more," and the freedom that comes from choosing yourself, even when it means leaving someone behind.

Yet, beyond the pain, this is also a story of strength—a story of a daughter who fought for connection, who extended lifeline after lifeline to a father who would not change, and who finally found peace by letting go. It's about the complicated love we can hold for people who hurt us, the aching hope that things might have been different, and the life that flourishes in their absence. It's about becoming whole, not because of them, but in spite of them.

I hope this story resonates with you the way Mean always has with me—an ode to resilience, self-discovery, and the quiet, radiant power of choosing to thrive.

Peace, Love, and Inspiration,

Britt Wolfe

The Invisible Girl

The air smelled of cut grass and asphalt, warm from the sun, the familiar end-of-summer scent that always marked the start of the school year in Jim Thorpe, Pennsylvania. Lina adjusted the strap of her backpack and stepped out of the car, feeling the late-August heat settle on her skin like an extra layer she couldn't shake.

Jim Thorpe Area High School loomed in front of her, red brick and sharp angles, the glass front doors reflecting the blue sky in a way that made the whole building seem impassable. Freshman year. Ninth grade. A new beginning, she told herself, even though she knew better. There were no fresh starts in a town where everyone had known you since kindergarten. There was no reinvention when you lived in a house where your father and older sister had already decided who you were with no input from you.

"Come on," Michelle called over her shoulder, not bothering to wait as she climbed out of the SUV. She moved ahead effortlessly, her honey-blonde hair catching the sunlight, her strides long and confident. Michelle was the kind of girl who took up space, not just physically but in a way that made everyone want to move closer. She could pull you in with a glance, make you feel special for a second before flicking you away like an afterthought.

Their father, Arlo, sat in the driver's seat of the old Ford Explorer, sunglasses perched on his nose. He didn't turn around. "Don't forget, Lini, you got that choir thing after school, right?"

Lina flinched at the nickname—Lini, the one her mother used to call her, the one that sounded wrong when Arlo said it. But she nodded. "Yeah."

"Michelle will wait for you after. You girls can walk home together."

Michelle sighed, but her voice was sweet when she answered. "Of course, Dad." The lie rolled off her tongue like it cost her nothing.

"Good girl," Arlo said, his voice full of warmth that was only ever directed at his eldest daughter.

Lina waited, just for a second, to see if he'd say it to her, too. He didn't.

The door slammed shut, and the SUV rumbled away, leaving a swirl of dust in its wake.

Michelle was already gone, absorbed into a cluster of girls near the doors. Lina didn't try to catch up. There was no point.

Lina didn't belong in Michelle's world. Not here. Not anywhere.

Inside, the hallways were already thick with movement—backpacks slung over shoulders, sneakers squeaking against polished floors, the air electric with the chaos of the first day. The walls, lined with red-and-black banners, screamed Jim Thorpe Olympians in bold white letters, the school mascot—a roaring lion—painted in exaggerated ferocity near the entrance to the gym.

Lina kept her head down, stepping carefully around clusters of students as she made her way to her locker. The numbers on the metal doors were worn, chipped at the edges from years of nervous hands twisting combination locks.

Her locker was next to a row of sophomores, laughing loudly as they exchanged stories from summer. Lina took a deep breath and turned the dial, counting each click in her head.

Thirty-two. Sixteen. Four.

She tugged at the handle, but it didn't budge.

Of course.

She tried again, slower this time, her fingers already sweaty against the cold metal.

"You sure that's your locker?" someone to her right snickered, and heat crawled up Lina's neck. She knew better than to look. She already recognized the voice—Jenna Madison, one of Michelle's friends.

Jenna leaned against the lockers, twirling a strand of dark hair around her finger, her lips already curved into the start of a smirk. "Maybe you should ask your big sister for help," she said, feigning concern before turning back to her group of friends, dissolving into laughter that Lina felt more than heard.

She ignored them, focused on the lock, turning the dial deliberately.

Thirty-two. Sixteen. Four.

The latch gave way, the metal door swinging open with a reluctant creak. Lina exhaled, placing her books inside, but she could still feel the heat of their eyes on her back.

She kept moving.

The rest of the day blurred together in a series of forgettable moments. Teachers handed out syllabi, students found their places in the social hierarchy, and the halls pulsed with the energy of teenagers adjusting to another year of the same thing.

Lina moved through it quietly, unnoticed, a shadow in a world too bright for her. This was the way she liked it. At just 14, she had perfected being a wallflower.

At lunch, she sat at the edge of a table occupied by other freshmen, nodding along to their conversation without contributing much. It was easier that way. Easier to let them talk over her than to try and force her way in.

She saw Michelle across the cafeteria, laughing with her friends, stealing fries from someone's tray like she owned the whole world. Lina looked away before their eyes could meet.

Her after school extracurricular—choir—was the only part of the day that felt like hers.

The music room smelled like old wood and freshly printed sheet music, the grand piano in the corner a reminder that there was something beautiful in this school.

Lina had always loved to sing. It was one of the few things that felt natural, like a part of her mother that still lived on inside of her. When she sang, she wasn't invisible. She wasn't someone's little sister. She was just Lina. Choir was the thing she looked forward to most about the start of the school year.

When rehearsal ended, the sun had already dipped below the tree line, painting the sky in bruised purples and soft oranges. The hallways were mostly empty, the last stragglers wrapping up their own extracurriculars and heading to their rides.

Lina hoisted her backpack onto her shoulder and stepped outside.

The school's grounds were dim, illuminated only by the streetlights that flickered with the buzzing hum of insects. She scanned the area, looking for Michelle's familiar figure. They were supposed to meet on the school front steps.

Nothing.

Lina shifted on her feet, her stomach knotting. Maybe Michelle was just late. Maybe she had gotten caught up in something. Lina was trying to convince herself of this, though she knew that wasn't the case.

She pulled out her phone and typed a quick text to her older sister: *Where are you?*

No response.

Minutes passed.

The school doors suddenly locked behind her with a mechanical click, the sound sending a shiver up her spine. The lock meant Michelle wasn't inside waiting somewhere.

Lina swallowed. She knew Michelle wasn't coming.

The walk home wasn't far, just under two miles, but the weight of the day settled heavy in her chest as she set off down the sidewalk.

Her backpack dug into her shoulders, her feet aching in her too-new sneakers, the air thick with the lingering scent of summer pavement and freshly cut grass. The town was quiet at this hour, only the occasional car passing, headlights sweeping over her before disappearing into the dark.

She told herself she wasn't upset. That it didn't matter.

But it did.

By the time she reached their house, the front porch light was already on. Arlo's car sat in the driveway. He was already home from work.

She climbed the steps and pushed open the door, stepping into the warmth of the house. The scent of takeout lingered in the air—probably Chinese, judging by the crumpled bag on the counter.

"Where were you?" Arlo's voice came from the kitchen, his tone casual, like he hadn't remembered Lina had been at choir.

"I—"

The door swung open behind her, and Michelle strolled in, her hair wind-tousled, the distinct smell of weed clinging to her clothes. She dropped her bag by the stairs and stretched like she had spent the afternoon doing something exhausting.

Lina's pulse spiked.

"Where were you?" she asked, her voice sharp before she could temper it.

Michelle turned to her, brow arching in practiced innocence. "What do you mean?"

"You were supposed to wait with me and walk home with me."

Michelle blinked, tilting her head. "I did wait for you," she said, voice syrupy sweet. "But you stormed off. Said you wanted to walk by yourself."

Lina felt the air punch out of her lungs. "What?"

Michelle shrugged. "I waited. I saw you walk away. Maybe you forgot, but you weren't exactly in a talking mood."

Lina turned to Arlo who had stepped out of the kitchen to see what was going on. "She's lying," she said, her voice thin, desperate. "She wasn't there. I texted her. She never answered. She—"

"That's enough," Arlo interrupted, his voice sharp in a way that brokered no argument.

Lina snapped her mouth shut.

"You're not going to fight with your sister over this." He sighed, rubbing a hand over his face like Lina was the exhausting one. "I don't know what's gotten into you, Lina, but this behaviour isn't acceptable. Lying isn't acceptable."

"I'm not lying!" Lina's voice cracked.

Arlo's eyes narrowed. "Enough. If this is how you're going to act, then maybe choir isn't a good fit for you."

Lina's stomach dropped.

No.

"But dad," she started, stepping forward, but he held up a hand.

"I don't want to hear it," he said, already turning back toward the living room. "You're done with choir. End of discussion."

Lina's mouth opened, then closed.

Michelle gave her a small, satisfied smile.

Lina turned on her heel and fled up the stairs, her throat tight, her chest aching.

Her room was the only place that felt safe. The only space in the entire world that belonged to her.

She closed the door softly behind her, pressing her forehead against the wood for a long moment before turning.

Sophie lifted her head from the bed, stretching languidly before hopping down, her small paws making no sound as she padded toward Lina. The Siamese cat blinked up at her with deep blue eyes, her tail curling around Lina's ankle.

Lina let out a shuddering breath and scooped her up, burying her face in her soft fur.

"At least you love me," she whispered, her voice breaking.

Sophie let out a small chirp of a meow, pressing her warm body into Lina.

Lina carried her to the bed and curled up beneath the covers, stroking her sleek fur with slow, even movements. The purring vibrating against her ribs.

"I don't understand what I did wrong," Lina murmured.

She felt so small, so insignificant, like a footnote in someone else's story.

She tried so hard to be good. To be kind. To be worthy of love. But no matter what she did, she was never enough.

Not for Arlo. Not for Michelle.

She could hear them downstairs, their laughter mingling with the opening credits of *Last Man Standing*. The theme music swelled, familiar and distant, wrapping around their easy conversation like a soundtrack to a life she wasn't part of.

It didn't feel fair.

Tears slipped down Lina's cheeks, hot and silent.

"I miss Mom," she whispered, pressing her lips to Sophie's fur. "She would have believed me about Michelle."

Sophie's purring didn't falter.

Lina swallowed hard.

She wondered what it would feel like to just... disappear. To step outside one night and keep walking, past the edges of town, past the places where people knew her name, until there was nothing left of her to miss, not that her father, or Michelle would miss her, or even notice she was gone.

The thought was dangerous, heavy, something she never let herself linger on for too long.

But tonight, it was there.

Sophie let out a soft, insistent meow, nudging her face against Lina's chin. Lina tightened her arms around her beloved cat, holding her close.

"I won't leave you," she promised.

And for now, that was enough.

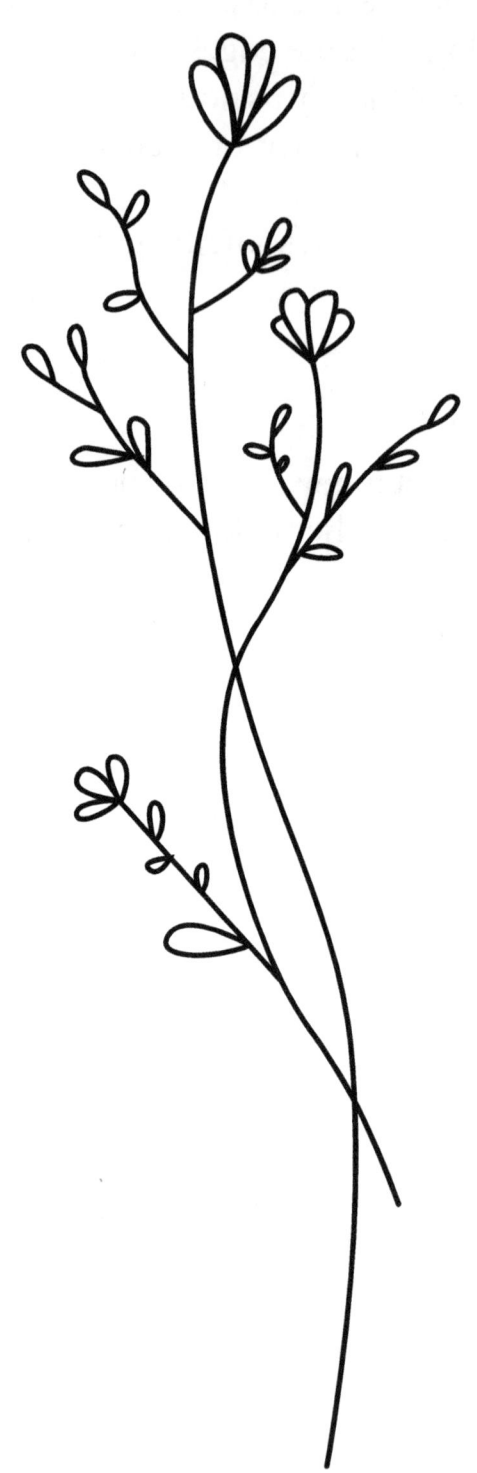

The house was always cold now.

It wasn't just the Pennsylvania winter creeping through the old windows, slipping through the cracks in the foundation, or lingering in the corners where the heat never quite reached. It was in the air itself, in the weight of silence that had settled thick and unshakable.

Lina had grown used to the quiet, to the way her father barely spoke to her unless he had to. It had been like this since Michelle left for Lehigh University—her third attempt at her first year. Her third chance, fully funded by their father, including rent for her off-campus apartment, textbooks she never read, and tuition for classes she barely attended. The money poured into Michelle's future like water down a drain, but Arlo never seemed to care.

Meanwhile, Lina sat at the chipped kitchen table, a half-empty coffee cup cooling beside her, reading through the acceptance letter she had yet to tell him about.

She ran her fingers over the thick paper, tracing the bold black letters at the top: Western Washington University. She had chosen it carefully—a place on the farthest edge of the country, in a town where the ocean stretched wide and endless. A place where she could breathe, where she could start over and invent herself free of the judgement of her father and older sister. A place where she could finally be free of this house and the family who had never really seen her.

A key rattled in the front door. Lina stiffened, clutching the acceptance letter in her hand as the door swung open. Arlo stepped inside, shaking the cold from his jacket, his face lined with exhaustion. His thinning hair was unkempt, his eyes bloodshot—not from work, because he didn't work, not anymore.

"How was your day?" she asked, more out of habit than expectation.

Arlo grunted in response, kicking off his boots and shuffling past her without so much as a glance.

That was their routine. She would ask. He would ignore her. The house would stay cold.

Lina clenched her jaw, staring down at her hands. The ache in her chest was familiar, expected. Still, it burned. Still, there was a part of her that wished it could be different.

From upstairs, the muffled meow of Sophie broke the silence. Lina exhaled slowly, pushing back from the table.

She climbed the stairs two at a time, her footsteps light against the worn hardwood. The door to her room was half-closed, and when she nudged it open, Sophie was already waiting on the bed, her sleek Siamese fur catching the dim glow of the bedside lamp.

"Hey, beautiful girl," Lina murmured, sitting on the edge of the mattress. Sophie stretched, arching her back before pressing her small body against Lina's side. For a moment, she let herself sink into the warmth, into the steady purr vibrating against her ribs. She ran a hand over Sophie's soft fur, staring at the letter that was still clenched in her fingers.

She had to tell him. She wanted to tell him. She wanted him to be happy for her. For a moment, Lina let herself envision a world where she bounded down the stairs, held out the acceptance letter and Arlo was pleased, excited and proud of his youngest daughter. In this dream world, he was even a little saddened that she would be leaving.

Filled with the warmth of her fantasy, Lina stood, clutching the letter like a lifeline as she made her way back downstairs. Arlo was in the living room now, sprawled in his recliner, a blanket draped over his lap. The TV flickered with the soft glow of an old rerun of *Star Trek: The Next Generation*, one of her father's all-time favourite television shows.

She lingered in the doorway, heart hammering.

"Dad?" She finally mustered the courage to say.

He didn't look away from the screen.

She swallowed hard. "I got into Western Washington University."

Silence from Arlo. The only sound was the low murmur of Captain Picard's voice, issuing some grave command to the crew of *The Enterprise*.

Lina tightened her grip on the letter. "It's in Bellingham. Right on the coast. They have a really good marketing and communications program."

Arlo exhaled, finally shifting to look at her. His eyes flickered to the paper in her hands, disinterest flashing across his face before he turned back to the television. "And?"

Lina's stomach dropped. "And... I'm going. In the fall."

Arlo nodded, as if she had just told him it might rain tomorrow. "Good for you."

Something in Lina's chest twisted. The realization crashed over her, swift and brutal. He didn't care. Not about her acceptance. Not about where she was going. Not about what she would study. She cursed herself for getting her hopes up that this moment in her life meant something to her own father, but she could have told him she was moving to another country, and it wouldn't have mattered.

She tried one more time. "It's... expensive," she said carefully.

Arlo let out a short, humourless laugh. "I'm not paying for it." The finality in his voice was absolute.

Lina swallowed against the lump rising in her throat.

"Not even a little?" she asked, hating the way the words trembled, hating the way she still hoped, even now.

Arlo sighed, finally turning to face her fully. His expression was unreadable. "Michelle is in school. I have no income right now. I can't afford both of you."

Michelle.

Of course.

The same Michelle who had failed out of her first year twice already. The same Michelle who was currently blowing through their father's money while barely scraping by in her third attempt at freshman year. The same

Michelle who spent most of her nights snorting cocaine in her off-campus apartment, sending frantic texts to Arlo when she needed more rent money.

And he still chose her at the expense of his youngest daughter.

Lina's hands clenched into fists. "You don't even care that I got in, do you?" she asked, her voice sharp, breaking at the edges.

Arlo rolled his eyes. "I said good for you, didn't I?"

"That's not the same as caring," Lina snapped.

Arlo sighed, rubbing a hand over his face. "Jesus, Lina, why do you always have to make everything so dramatic?"

She let out a sharp, bitter laugh. "You think I'm dramatic? You refuse to see me, and I'm the dramatic one?"

Arlo groaned, turning back toward the TV after another condescending eye roll. "This conversation is over."

No. Not this time. Lina stepped forward, her pulse hammering in her ears. "You bought Michelle a car," she said, voice shaking. "You're paying for her rent. You're paying for her classes, even though she's failing again."

Arlo's jaw tightened.

"You won't even buy my graduation photos," she continued, her voice rising. "You made me buy my own dress for senior prom. You said I was lucky you still paid for my school supplies, but you would rather go broke paying for Michelle's third attempt at school—"

"Enough." His voice was low, sharp. A warning.

Lina shook her head. "You don't even know me," she whispered. "You don't want to know me."

Arlo exhaled heavily, running a hand through his thinning grey hair. "Go away, Lina."

She stared at him, waiting for something—an apology, a look of regret, anything. But he just turned the volume up on the TV, Captain Picard's voice filling the room, drowning her out completely.

Lina turned and walked away.

Upstairs, Sophie was waiting for her, perched on her pillow, her blue eyes blinking in the dim light. Lina crawled into bed, pulling the blankets up to her chin as she curled around the small, warm weight of her cat.

Sophie meowed softly, pressing her nose to Lina's cheek. "I wish you were my dad," Lina murmured into her fur.

Sophie purred, her presence steady and warm.

Lina tightened her arms around her, blinking back tears.

"I just wanted him to be proud of me," she whispered into Sophie's fur. Sophie only purred louder, as if trying to drown out the pain.

Lina closed her eyes.

The house was cold. It always had been, but tonight, it seeped into her bones, into the hollow space in her chest where love should have been. Her father's rejection clung to her like frostbite, numbing, relentless. She had tried—God, she had tried—to be enough, to be someone worth seeing, worth choosing, worth loving. But maybe she never would be. Maybe there was something broken in her, something so fundamentally unlovable that even her own father couldn't find space for her in his heart. The thought curled inside her like smoke, dark and suffocating, and for a fleeting, terrible moment, she wondered if the ache of being invisible would ever stop—if it would ever matter if she was here at all.

But then Sophie stirred against her chest, letting out a soft, sleepy sigh, pressing her small body closer. Lina clung to the warmth, to the steady rhythm of her purring, to the only proof that something in this world still needed her.

As Lina drifted off to sleep, she wished her mother was here and wondered how different things would be if she hadn't passed away a decade ago.

Still Something To Prove
Four Years Later

Lina had built a life without her father.

She had worked herself to the bone for it—balancing full-time coursework with full-time jobs, pulling espresso shots at dawn and editing marketing proposals until midnight, stretching every dollar so she wouldn't have to ask anyone for help. Not from her father. Not from Michelle.

And now, in just a few weeks, she and Sam would be leaving it all behind. The tiny apartment in Bellingham, the early morning walks to class, the brief moments of togetherness between work and study. They were moving to Newcastle, New South Wales—to a place where the ocean stretched wide and endless, where the air smelled like salt and possibility, where they could start a life near Sam's family.

The day Lina met Sam, the sky was cloudless, the waves lapping at the shore in lazy, rolling curls. It was late May, the air still crisp with the last breath of spring, but warm enough that she had kicked off her sandals to feel the sand between her toes as she studied at an ocean-side café.

She sat—her marketing textbook open in front of her, the pages curling slightly in the salty breeze—when a shadow fell over her table.

"You look like you could use another cup of coffee."

Lina glanced up.

Sam stood there, holding a steaming paper cup, his dark blonde hair windswept, his grey-blue eyes crinkling at the corners as he smiled. His voice—deep, smooth, Australian—sent a strange warmth through her.

"I—I didn't order another one," Lina said, blinking up at him.

"I know," he said, setting it down in front of her. "But you've been staring at that same page for at least ten minutes, and I figured caffeine might help."

Lina stared at the cup, then back at him.

Sam grinned. "I work here, by the way. I'm not just some guy handing out free coffee to strangers."

Lina laughed—really laughed—for the first time in what felt like forever. She was taken by his charm, his easy confidence, the way he dropped every single 'r' he should have pronounced. There was something about him that felt light, like sunshine after a long winter.

And they had been inseparable ever since.

Sam had moved into Lina's apartment less than a month later, and though Sophie had been slow to accept him—hissing, stalking around him like he was an invader—eventually, even she had curled up in his lap, purring.

The three of them had become a family. A small, happy, chosen family.

Lina had spent so much of her life fighting to be seen, to be acknowledged, to be worth something. And yet, now, as she curled her fingers around her phone, her thumb hovering over her father's number, she felt the same gnawing dread she always had before speaking to him.

Some wounds didn't heal, no matter how much distance she put between them.

"You don't have to ask for anything," Sam had told her earlier that evening, his grey-blue eyes soft with understanding. "But he should know. You deserve to tell him, let him know what you have accomplished in spite of him."

Lina wasn't sure she agreed, but still, she pressed call on her cell phone.

The phone rang twice before Arlo picked up. "What?" he said though bites of something crunchy he couldn't pull himself away from. There was no hello. No recognition that he hadn't heard from her in months.

Lina swallowed. "Hey, Dad."

She barely had time to process his usual disinterest before a second voice cut through the line—sharp, familiar, cruel.

"Who is it?" Michelle demanded, her voice rough and ragged, as if she had spent a lifetime shouting or smoking too much. It was definitely the latter.

Arlo sighed. "Lina."

"Oh, great," Michelle scoffed, her voice getting closer. "What, did she finally run out of money and need something?"

Lina felt her stomach turn. "I don't need anything," she said, her voice steady. "I was calling to let you know that I'm graduating soon."

Silence.

Then, a sharp, incredulous laugh. "No, you're not," Michelle said, her tone dripping with condescension. "You didn't actually finish anything. Stop making shit up."

Lina's jaw clenched. "Yes, I did."

Michelle snorted. "You're such a liar. The only way you could have finished school is if you bought a degree. I see your Instagrams all the time—you work at a coffee shop full-time and hang out at the beach. Tell me, when exactly have you done all this supposed studying to finish university?" Her voice dripped with condescension, every word laced with the smug certainty of someone who had never accomplished anything but still considered herself an expert on everyone else's life.

The irony was almost laughable. Michelle, who had flunked out of Lehigh University three times and whose only so-called academic achievement was one of those meaningless, TV-advertised courses, had the audacity to accuse Lina of lying.

Lina exhaled slowly, forcing herself to stay calm. She didn't need to convince her sister. She didn't need to justify herself. "I didn't call to argue with you."

"Then why did you call?" Arlo muttered between bites of whatever he was eating. Crackers, by the sound of it. Lina could practically see him in his recliner, a box of Ritz balanced on his gut, crumbs spilling down his shirt in a lazy dusting of processed cheese powder and self-neglect.

Lina shut her eyes. She should have known better. Of course she should have known better than to expect her father to care what his youngest daughter is doing. "Because after graduation, Sam and I are moving to Australia."

A beat of silence. Then Michelle snorted. "Oh, please," she scoffed. "You? Moving to Australia? Sure, Lina. You're so full of it."

"I'm not lying," Lina snapped before she could stop herself.

Michelle let out an exaggerated sigh, her voice dropping into a low, guttural growl. "Don't talk back to me." Then, to their father: "See, Dad? This is why I should've beat the shit out of her more as a kid. She never learned respect."

Lina's breath caught. She couldn't see the link between her announcement and Michelle's obsession with violence and respect. The disconnect was so painfully obvious, so absurd, that she knew—she knew—her father had to see it, too.

Arlo said nothing. As always, he let Michelle's words sit in the air, thick and poisonous, unchecked.

Lina felt something inside her tighten, something deep and hot and unbearable. "Respect?" she asked, her voice shaking with rage. "I'll respect you when there's something to respect."

Michelle inhaled sharply. And then—"You selfish, self-involved bitch!" she shrieked. There was a rustling sound, a clatter, the muffled wail of a child. Lina didn't need to be there to see it—she could picture it perfectly. Michelle yanking her son into her arms, storming around in a grand performance of victimhood.

"I can't deal with her right now," Michelle sobbed. "Come on, Andrew, we're leaving," Michelle proclaimed as Andrew cried. A door slammed. Silence.

Then Arlo's voice came, low and furious. "What the hell is wrong with you?" He demanded.

Lina blinked. "Excuse me?"

Arlo exhaled sharply, the sound heavy with exhaustion—as if she was the one exhausting him. "She's your sister, Lina. How dare you talk to her like that?"

Lina clenched her teeth. "She just told you—right to your face—that she should've beaten me more when we were kids. And you're mad at me? She accused me of lying, insulted me, and you said nothing."

"Oh, don't be so dramatic," Arlo muttered. That was all he ever said when she called out the way her father and sister treated her. Every time. Every. Single. Time.

"You always get so hysterical," he added, with the same irritated tone he always used whenever she tried to stand up for herself.

Something inside Lina snapped again. "She's always been like this," she said, her voice rising. "And you let her. You always let her. She could say anything – she could say anything to me and you'd still take her side."

Arlo sighed, that same tired, exasperated sigh he had given her since childhood. And then, with chilling finality—"You are a self-involved bitch, Lina. You always have been."

Lina felt like she had been punched. Her fingers went numb around her phone. She had spent years—years—trying to prove she was good enough. Good enough to be noticed. Good enough to be seen.

But here he was, her own father, telling her exactly what he thought of her.

She opened her mouth, grasping for something—anything—to say, but before she could, the line went dead.

He had hung up on her.

The phone slipped from her fingers, clattering onto the coffee table. Sam was already moving, already pulling her into his arms as the first tear slid down her cheek. "I hate him," Sam murmured into her hair, his voice thick with rage. "I hate him."

Lina didn't answer.

Her body shook, the weight of years pressing into her bones, settling into the spaces her father's love had never filled. Sam pulled away just long enough to grab his phone from the armrest of their worn couch. Out of the corner of her eye, Lina saw the screen glow—his messages open, her father's number already pulled up.

She grabbed his wrist, shaking her head. "Don't," she whispered.

Sam's jaw tightened. "Lina—"

"We're leaving in a few weeks," she reminded him. "It doesn't matter. Just... let it go."

Sam exhaled through his nose, his grip tightening on the phone. Then, reluctantly, he locked the screen and set it aside, settling himself back onto the couch. Lina curled into his chest, Sophie hopping up beside them. The cat nestled against her, purring softly, the only steady sound in the room.

Lina closed her eyes. For so long, she had fought to be seen. To be something to Arlo. To Michelle. But finally, she realized—She didn't have to fight anymore. Not for them, and not for the love that should be given freely, not wielded to hurt and harm.

Eight years in Newcastle had settled into Lina's bones, softening the raw edges of her past like sea glass smoothed by the tide. The salt air, the slow rise and fall of the Pacific, the stretch of sand beneath her bare feet—this place had become home in a way that Jim Thorpe, and even Bellingham, never had.

She had built a life here, a real one. Sam had completed his retraining and was thriving as a graphic designer, working from their sunlit home office that overlooked the backyard garden they had painstakingly built together. Lina, now a highly sought-after marketing executive, had reached a point where she could work selectively, choosing the projects that excited her rather than the ones that simply paid the bills. They had carved out a world filled with warmth, love, success and the steady hum of happiness.

Sophie, older now but still as regal and possessive as ever, lounged in her favourite spot by the window, watching the street below like a self-appointed queen of their quiet corner of Newcastle.

For a long time, Lina had left the past behind. It was a choice. A deliberate, intentional untying of the knots that had once bound her to the family she had left after her mom passed away: Michelle and Arlo. She had learned to stop reaching for something that would never be given to her.

And yet, at some point, she had been the one to reach out again.

She wasn't sure what had compelled her to do it. Maybe it was Sam, gently reminding her that people could change. Maybe it was the nagging whispers of guilt that had never fully left her, the small voice that still wanted to believe that surely, surely, her father must have loved her in his own way.

Rebuilding their relationship had been slow, awkward. Arlo had never apologized—not in so many words—but he had answered when she called. He had asked about her life, and for the first time, he had listened. It was surface-level at first, but then he and his new wife, Katrina, had come to visit, and for a little while, Lina had let herself believe that maybe things had changed.

Maybe, at long last, she had a father.

The trip had been Lina's idea—an extravagant Christmas gift, a gesture of goodwill, a hope wrapped in airline tickets. Arlo and Katrina had never been to Australia, had never left the United States, in fact, and Lina had thought—what better way to mend what had always been broken than to offer him something unforgettable?

She had pictured her father standing on Merewether Beach, the golden sunlight casting long shadows over the surf, the ocean stretching wide and endless before him. Maybe, in that moment, he would see her—not as Michelle's shadow, not as the difficult, dramatic, undeserving daughter— but as someone worth knowing.

And for a little while, it had been good.

They had walked along the coastline, Katrina snapping photos with an iPad held at an awkward angle. Arlo had grumbled about the heat but had smiled, real and easy, when Sam pointed out a pod of dolphins cresting the waves. They had cooked meals together, shared long lunches on the

back patio, let the soft rhythm of life in Newcastle fold them in.
But there had been cracks.

Katrina had always been odd—prickly, passive-aggressive in the way
people were when they thought they were being subtle. She had accused
Lina of hiding the remote control—of all things—when it turned up
between the couch cushions an hour later. She had insisted on organizing
a group hike one afternoon, though no one had asked her to, then sulked
the entire time and claimed her knees were permanently damaged from
the "unexpected incline," eventually tossing her water bottle into the
bushes in a theatrical display of defeat.

Sam and Lina had planned a surprise lunch at one of Newcastle's famous
restaurants, a place that served kangaroo, a local delicacy. Katrina had
stared at them as if they had slapped her across the face.

"We don't like eating out," she had declared, arms folded tightly across her
chest.

The tension had been there, simmering beneath the surface, but Lina had
ignored it. She had learned to ignore so many things.

What she had not ignored—what had settled in the back of her mind like
an itch she couldn't quite scratch—was the way Arlo never corrected
Katrina. Never told her to stop treating his daughter the way she was,
never stepped in when she crossed the line.

He had never stood up for Lina and he never would.

It wasn't until weeks after they had returned home that the call had come.

It had started fine, casual even. Arlo had asked about work, about Sam, about how Sophie was adjusting after her "horrific experience of having strangers in her home." Lina had laughed at that. It had been easy, comfortable.

Then, somehow, the shift.

Lina had said something about Sam handling most of the cooking while she worked late hours—an offhand comment, a nothing statement. But Arlo had latched onto it.

"You make him do too much," he had said.

Lina had paused. "What?"

"He does all the cooking?" Arlo scoffed, as if she had just confessed to running a sweatshop out of their home. "Christ, Lina. The man needs space to be a man, and you've got him slaving away in the kitchen? You make him do too much."

Lina's pulse had kicked up. "Sam likes to cook, Dad. And he does the cooking because I work sixty hours a week. We're a team."

Arlo had let out a long, beleaguered sigh. "All I'm saying is that a man shouldn't have to—"

And that's when she knew.

The words, the tone—it wasn't him. It was Michelle.

It was always Michelle.

Lina had gone still, pressing the phone tighter against her ear, the warmth of her father's voice gone cold. "Dad," she had said, carefully measured.

"Where is this coming from?"

A pause. Then: "What do you mean?"

"You didn't care about Sam doing the cooking when you were here. You didn't say anything about it then."

"Yeah, well," Arlo muttered. "I've been thinking about it. About how, when your mother was alive, I'd come home from work and she'd just be on me. Nagging. Complaining. Just like you."

Lina stilled. The words struck like a slap, sharp and deliberate. This wasn't new. He had launched this attack before, dissecting her mother's memory with the casual cruelty of a man who had never learned to shoulder his own failings. He had always framed it the same way—how he had been the breadwinner, how he had taken care of everything while her mother had done nothing but stayed home.

Of course, Arlo had never seen the work her mother had done. He hadn't noticed the way the house had stayed clean, the groceries had been stocked, the meals had appeared on the table. He hadn't thought about the school runs, the doctor's appointments, the sacrifices that made their world run smoothly—until the day they stopped.

He had never acknowledged that she had worked before the cancer took her. He had only seen what she wasn't once she became too sick to carry the weight of an entire household alone.

And Michelle—Michelle had inherited that same bitter narrative. Her memories of their mother had been rewritten into something cruel, something twisted. To her, their mother had been nothing but a woman who took advantage of her husband, who let him shoulder everything financially, while she did nothing.

Lina's stomach twisted, the sickness of it curling inside her like something living, something familiar. He had been fed something—words slipped into his ear like poison from the only voice he had ever trusted. He and Michelle fed off each other, their revisionist history growing sharper, uglier, more pointed with time. Their hatred for her mother had become something shared, and their comparison of Lina to her had never been anything but deliberate and intended to hurt.

Aimed to wound.

And Lina had let her guard down. She should have known. She should have expected it. But somehow, she had let herself believe.

Lina took a slow, steadying breath, staring out the window at the gentle sway of the palm trees, at the ocean beyond, its waves rolling in with the same ceaseless rhythm they always had. "Dad," she said, her voice quieter now, tired in a way that had nothing to do with the late hour. "Have you been talking to Michelle?"

Silence.

And there it was.

It didn't matter that she hadn't spoken to Michelle in years. It didn't matter that she had never asked Arlo to choose between them. It didn't matter that she had spent a lifetime proving herself, clawing for a love that had never been freely given, only to be told—over and over—that she had already lost.

Michelle was still in his ear. And Lina? Lina would never be loud enough to be heard over her.

She felt it then, the old wound splitting open, raw and red-hot, tearing through her with the force of a truth she had always known but had tried so desperately to outrun. She had wanted to fight. To demand that he see her. To beg for the things she had always wanted from him.

But slowly, she was starting to learn and to know better.

The ocean stretched endlessly outside her window, vast and wild and free. She had spent years learning that she could leave.

Maybe it was time to remember how.

When Lina and Sam moved back to Pennsylvania, they settled in a town close enough to Jim Thorpe that visits to and from her father and Katrina were manageable, but far enough that she didn't have to live in the shadow of her past. It was supposed to be a fresh start, a way to balance having Arlo in her life without being consumed by the weight of his indifference.

Their home was a joyful refuge—tucked into a cul-de-sac on the edge of a sprawling wooded area, where the trees whispered in the wind and the scent of damp earth clung to the air. It wasn't Newcastle, but it was close to something like peace.

At first, it had seemed like the right decision. The right thing to do. Arlo was old now—really old, with thinning grey hair and a slow shuffle to his gait. He was overweight, hunched slightly as if the years had physically pressed down on him. His teeth, what remained of them, were yellowed and stained from age and decades of bad coffee. He moved with a kind of carelessness, a man who had been given every privilege but had done nothing with it. And yet, Lina worried that when he died, she would regret not having tried harder at their father-daughter relationship. That the guilt would consume her the way his disinterest always had.

So, every Wednesday night, she cooked for him and Katrina.

She told herself it was an olive branch. A way to start fresh. And for a while, it almost worked. Arlo would show up, Katrina clinging to his arm like a barnacle, her too-young skin stretched tight over a face that was always slightly sneering. She wore too much makeup and spoke too loudly, filling the room with complaints about her consulting business.

"You both are just so lucky," Katrina would say, waving a dismissive hand at Lina and Sam. "People just hand success to some folks. It's got nothing to do with talent."

Lina would bite the inside of her cheek, Sam's hand finding hers beneath the table. Katrina's 'business' was supposedly some kind of consulting firm, but in reality, it was nothing more than a Facebook page and a string of unpaid invoices. She spent her days arguing with strangers on the internet, crafting long-winded posts about personal responsibility while living off Arlo's dwindling pension. Lina had tried—God, she had tried—to give her real, actionable advice. But Katrina never wanted advice. She wanted sympathy. She wanted excuses.

And Arlo.

Arlo would sit back, eating the meals Lina cooked without a word of thanks. But at the end of every dinner, he would turn to Sam, pat his shoulder, and say, "Thanks for dinner, Sam." Every single time.

Sam would tense beside her. Lina could feel it, the way his fingers tightened around his fork, the way his jaw clenched. But he never corrected Arlo. Never told him that it was Lina who spent hours planning and cooking. Because Lina had made it clear—this was easier. It was easier to take the insult than to fight for something that would never come.

"It's just words," she told Sam one night after the couple had left.

"No, it's not," he said, standing at the sink, scrubbing plates with too much force. "It's every fucking week, Lina."

Lina swallowed, glancing at Sophie, curled up on the windowsill, watching them with her usual silent judgment. She sighed, stepping forward to take Sam's hand, stilling his movements. "I just don't want to fight him."

Sam exhaled sharply through his nose. "You shouldn't have to fight to be seen by your own father." He was right. Of course he was right. But what was the alternative? If she let go, if she cut Arlo out of her life completely, there would be no more second chances. No more 'maybe one days.'

And she wasn't sure she was ready for that yet.

The weeks passed. The same routine. The same quiet cuts that built up like a thousand tiny wounds. Lina tried to befriend Katrina. She truly did. She asked her about her business, about her interests. She tried to find common ground. But Katrina wasn't interested in friendship. She was interested in pity.

"My business is struggling because people don't want to take advice from someone who knows more than them," she complained one night, swirling cheap wine in her glass. "Everyone is so threatened by intelligence."

Lina opened her mouth to suggest that perhaps Katrina should spend less time arguing with strangers on the internet and more time actually working, but she stopped herself. What was the point? Katrina didn't want to hear it, wouldn't accept the advice and it would just cause a rift.

And Arlo.

Arlo continued to do what he did best—nothing. He had been given every advantage in life. His parents had sent him to Yale, where he had flunked out halfway through his second year. He had coasted ever since, jumping from one failed venture to another, never truly working, always convinced that he was the smartest person in the room. He had taken an IQ test once, decades ago, and had qualified for Mensa. And in his mind, that was enough. He was brilliant. He was more brilliant than any other person in any room. He didn't need to prove it.

So he spent his days doing nothing. He sat. He napped. He watched reruns of *Star Trek: The Next Generation* while the house that had been Lina's childhood home fell apart around him.

And he criticized. Everything.

"It's just bullshit, really. What you guys do, I mean." He mused one evening, as Sam cleared the dinner plates. "Marketing isn't real work. It's just convincing people to buy into bullshit."

Sam froze mid-step, his fingers tightening around the plates. Lina placed a hand on his back, silently willing him to let it go. He did. But later that night, when they were alone in their house, Sam turned to her, his voice low, controlled.

"Lina, I don't want to do this anymore."

Lina knew what he meant. He wasn't asking for clarification. He wasn't making a suggestion. She swallowed, looking away. "I know."

But she wasn't ready yet. She wasn't ready to let go of Arlo, even if he had let go of her a long time ago.

And so, the dinners continued. The resentment built as they left Arlo unchecked in his barbed words and ignorance of his youngest daughter. And each time, Arlo left behind something heavier than the silence—proof that, no matter how hard she tried, no matter how much she bent and twisted herself into something palatable, something pleasing—he would never see her.

She would always be the daughter he tolerated. And for now, Lina accepted it.

Because someday, Arlo would be gone.

And she would have no reason to feel guilty for not trying. But, the trying was hard.

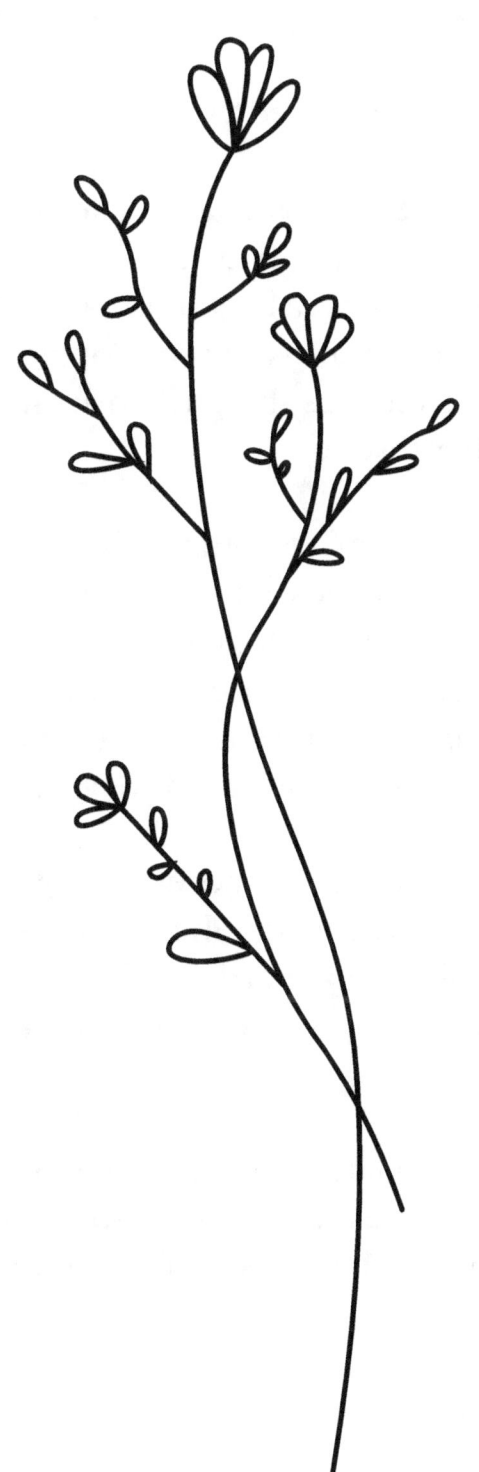

All You're Ever Going To Be Is Mean

Lina had everything she'd ever worked for.

She and Sam's marketing agency was soaring, climbing to heights she hadn't even dared to dream of. They had the kind of success that turned heads, the kind that afforded them a beautiful home, travel to sun-drenched destinations, and the ability to spoil Sophie with gourmet cat food and custom-made velvet beds she ignored in favour of the worn-out couch she'd claimed as her throne.

Lina had built a life of comfort, of adventure, of abundance. Yet, the ghost of her father still lurked in the edges of her happiness. Every week, she invited Arlo and Katrina to dinner, still clinging to the hope that she would one day feel something resembling the love a father is supposed to have for their daughter, that he would one day look at her and see someone worth knowing. Maybe, one day, he would even be proud of her.

But Arlo remained a hollow presence, more an obligation now than a father. Katrina, as ever, was exhausting. She was full of complaints—about her consulting business, about how hard it was to make money, about how lucky Lina and Sam were for their success, never mind how hard they had worked for it.

"It's not about talent," she would say over dinner, swirling wine in her glass with the air of someone who believed the world and fate had conspired against her. "Some people just have doors open for them. Others get locked out."

Sam would grip Lina's hand under the table, silently reminding himself not to react, for Lina's sake.

"You should just be grateful," Arlo had said once, when Sam had offhandedly mentioned that they were working long hours to keep up with their growing clientele. "Not everyone gets the kind of breaks you do."

Lina had nearly laughed. Breaks? As if their success had come from anything but their own relentless effort. As if she hadn't worked full-time while studying full-time, juggling a million responsibilities just to keep her head above water.

Arlo had never understood work. He had been given everything in life—an Ivy League education he had squandered, an easy ride through every failure, the luxury of never having to worry about money until it was too late. And yet, he still saw himself as an intellectual, as someone superior, as a man who should be revered. He thought of himself as a genius, still coasting on accolades he received as a child, though he had never accomplished much.

The weight of his condescension, his casual dismissiveness, the way he always found a way to diminish his daughter—it was wearing Lina down. And then, just as she was thinking about pulling away, the videos surfaced.

It started with a client.

"I hate to even bring this up," the woman had said, shifting uncomfortably over *Zoom*, her eyes darting away from the camera. "But there's... something I came across online. A TikToker has been posting about you. She claims to be your sister."

Lina's stomach sank...Michelle.

The woman hesitated before continuing, her voice carefully neutral. "She's saying some pretty awful things. Accusing you of being a narcissist, of using charity work to fuel some kind of... hero complex. That your charity efforts are actually designed to keep people sick and needing your help. I don't believe any of it, obviously. But it's gaining traction."

Lina's breath felt shallow.

"She made a forty-five-minute video," the woman added, almost apologetically. "Would you like me to send you the link?"

Sam, sitting next to Lina, answered for her. "Yes."

The moment the call ended, Sam opened the video. And there was Michelle. A heavy filter smoothed out her aging skin, her words were slightly distorted by a strange voice effect she'd used, but there was no mistaking the vitriol in her eyes, the deep-seated anger she had always carried. She was sitting in what was unmistakably their father's kitchen, a white refrigerator covered in old magnets visible behind her.

And she was ranting. Lina sat frozen as Michelle's voice rose with manufactured outrage, spiraling into a monologue of unhinged accusations.

"She's evil," Michelle seethed. "A narcissist. She doesn't care about people. All this charity work? It's a scam. She just wants to look good. She needs people to be sick and struggling so she can swoop in and act like she's some kind of saviour."

Lina's jaw clenched.

"She's never helped me," Michelle continued, her voice laced with self-pity.

"I've raised my son alone, with no help. Meanwhile, she's off on her little vacations, drinking fancy cocktails, living in luxury, while I struggle every day."

Sam let out a low exhale. "She has lived rent-free in your father's house for years," he muttered, pausing the video. "She's delusional." Lina just stared at the screen, numb.

There were more videos. Dozens of them. All filmed in the same kitchen, all the same ranting tirades. Michelle painting herself as a victim, rewriting history, distorting facts until she had created a version of reality where Lina was the villain.

And people were believing it.

In the comments, strangers debated whether Lina was an ungrateful, spoiled narcissist, or just a straight up sociopath. Some dug into Lina's LinkedIn, pulling details about her company. Others asked Michelle if she had proof, to which Michelle simply replied, "I lived it." Comments poured in offering Michelle support for her life of victimhood at the hands of her sister. The same sister Michelle had conveniently forgotten to mention she'd had nothing to do with for more than a decade.

Lina didn't respond.

She didn't post a rebuttal. Didn't reach out. Didn't acknowledge Michelle's existence. And still, the videos kept coming.

At the same time, Arlo was growing meaner.

At first, it was subtle. The usual barbs, the passive-aggressive commentary at dinner, the dismissive attitude. But then, one night, he brought up Michelle outright.

"She's upset with you," he said, stabbing at his mashed potatoes. "I don't know why you two can't just get along."

Lina tensed.

"I don't speak to Michelle," she said evenly.

"She's your sister," Arlo said, as if that alone meant something. "She loves you. She just wants to work things out."

Lina scoffed. "She's been making videos about me, Dad. Publicly attacking me. She's lying, and you know she's lying."

Arlo waved a hand. "You're both dramatic."

Lina set her fork down, suddenly sick to her stomach. "So, you believe her?"

"I don't want to be in the middle of this."

The conversation ended abruptly, Arlo and Katrina leaving in a huff.

Days later, a text arrived. It was from Arlo: *Michelle is really hurt by how you're treating her.*

Lina stared at the message, bile rising in her throat. She responded, keeping her words measured: *Michelle has been lying about me online for months, and I haven't even acknowledged her. If anyone should be hurt, it's me.*

Arlo's reply came instantly: *TL;DR*

Lina blinked. Really? He was going to be that overtly dismissive? That was shocking, even for her father.

Another message popped up: *I don't want to be in the middle of this.*

Lina's hands shook. There was no middle. There was nothing for him to be in the middle of.

She, Sam, and Sophie had been living their lives. Quietly. Peacefully. Happily. And Michelle had attacked her and continued to attack her.

Still, Arlo couldn't see Lina for who she was. He couldn't see past Michelle, past whatever twisted narrative she had spun. Through her fury and hurt, a memory climbed to the surface.

She remembered Katrina, when they'd come to visit in Australia, recounting a conversation she'd had with Arlo.

"I asked him why he talked about Michelle so much," Katrina had said, laughing. "I told him I'd never even heard him mention you." Lina had braced herself.

"You know what he told me?" Katrina had continued, eyes glinting with something cruel. "He said he just loved Michelle so much because she was his first-born. That was it. He just loves her more because she was first."

Lina had laughed at the time. It had been an ugly, bitter laugh, the kind that tasted like grief. Now, as she sat staring at her father's text, it wasn't funny, and it finally sunk in.

For so long, she had believed there was something wrong with her. That she was horrible. That she was no good. But it wasn't her that was flawed and broken. It was him.

Arlo was broken. Delusional about his youngest daughter. And she had wasted her entire life trying to prove her worth to a man who had never seen her at all, and didn't want to.

The Same Old Bitter Man

The first cease and desist order was sent on a crisp autumn morning, delivered by courier to Arlo's run down home where Michelle still lived. The letter had been carefully worded—formal, unshakable, warning of legal action if she did not remove the defamatory videos and cease her relentless attacks against Lina, Sam, and their business.

By the end of the day, Michelle had uploaded another TikTok. Once again her face was distorted by a heavy filter that smudged her harsh features, while her voice shrieked with a tone straight from the halls of an asylum . She held up the letter as if it were an award, her grin wide and manic.

"Would you look at this? My narcissistic bitch of a sister is threatening me! Can you believe this? Trying to silence me because she knows I'm telling the truth! Lina is a fraud, a manipulator, and a liar, and I will not be silenced."

Lina had felt her stomach drop, but Sam had simply leaned back in his chair, exhaled, and muttered, "Alright. We do this the hard way, then."

The lawsuit was filed within the week. Michelle, naturally, turned it into content.

"They think they can intimidate me," she ranted in one video, the bags under her eyes dark with exhaustion, a stark contrast to the cutesy heart filter floating around her face. "They think they can use their money to bully me, but I know my rights. I am a single mother fighting for my son, and I will never back down."

Michelle, of course, had never backed down from playing the victim.

She responded to the lawsuit with a flurry of counter-filings, most of which were incomprehensible gibberish. She flooded the court system with accusations—Lina and Sam were "abusing the legal system," they were "going against standard courtroom procedure," they were "trying to destroy a mother who had nothing."

Meanwhile, Michelle refused to properly serve Lina and Sam with the documents she was filing.

Instead, she posted TikToks about how she wasn't serving them. She cackled as she waved stacks of papers, boasting about how she had filed them but wasn't "legally obligated" to let them see what she had submitted.

"She's literally admitting to breaking procedural law," Sam said one night, staring at his phone in disbelief as Michelle continued to rant and rave.

Lina rubbed her temples. "She's too stupid to realize that." Watching Michelle's TikToks had become a joke between them. "It's so strange," Lina began, "She used to be smarter. I used to look up to her. I used to want to be her when we were kids." A frown settled on her face. "It's sad really," she said softly. "It didn't have to be like this. If dad had reined her in instead of letting her grow into this grotesque monster..." her words trailed off. She could no longer cling to alternate versions of reality.

For months, the court battle had been dragging on. Michelle missed deadlines and then accused Lina and Sam of missing deadlines. She arrived at hearings late, dressed in oversized hoodies and leggings, dark sunglasses shielding her puffy, sleep-deprived eyes.

In court, she contradicted herself at every turn. She was poor and helpless, but she was also a successful businesswoman. She had never said anything bad about Lina, except for the hundreds of videos where she called her a narcissist, a fraud, a thief, an abuser, a monster. She was intelligent and well-read, but she didn't understand why the court expected her to follow legal procedures. She was a victim, a warrior, a mother just trying to survive.

And through it all, Arlo said nothing. The only sign that he had any thoughts on the matter at all was a text he sent Sam out of nowhere one evening: *Bet you regret marrying a woman like that now.*

Sam had stared at the screen for a long moment, exhaled, then locked his phone without replying. Not yet.

By the time the final hearing rolled around, Michelle looked like a shell of a human being. She had spent the last few months railing against Lina, screaming into her phone at all hours, drowning in paranoia and rage. Her skin was dull, her eyes sunken, her once meticulously styled blonde hair now grown out into patchy, brittle strands of neglected roots.

And Lina? Lina had never looked or felt stronger.

She sat beside Sam in her sharp, tailored suit, her hands folded neatly on the desk in front of her, her expression unreadable. She wasn't scared of Michelle anymore. It had taken Lina her entire lifetime, but at last, she had gotten here, and it felt like freedom.

The judge's voice rang through the courtroom, final and absolute.

"I have reviewed the extensive evidence presented in this case, and it is abundantly clear that the defendant, Miss. Mayfield, has engaged in a prolonged and deliberate campaign of defamation and harassment against the plaintiffs, Mrs. Morgan and Mr. Morgan."

Michelle tensed as the judge continued, his tone steely.

"Miss. Mayfield, I have rarely encountered a defendant who so openly flaunts their contempt for the legal system, who weaponizes the judicial process while simultaneously claiming to be its victim. You have filed frivolous motions, ignored deadlines, and turned this courtroom into a stage for your own delusions. You have fabricated allegations, twisted facts, and attempted to paint yourself as an innocent party when, in reality, you have been the aggressor in this matter from the very beginning."

Michelle's lips parted, but the judge raised a hand, silencing her.

"Do not interrupt me." He said hotly. "In this room, I am the boss and you will listen to me. Not the other way around."

Michelle's mouth slapped shut.

The judge leaned forward, his expression stern. "I have watched you, Miss. Mayfield, attempt to gaslight an entire courtroom. I have seen you contradict yourself within minutes, shift blame, and present yourself as a helpless victim while openly admitting to the very actions you have been accused of. I have seen you attempt to manipulate legal proceedings the way you manipulate people, and I assure you, it has not worked."

Michelle's face had gone pale.

Lina could almost hear the cogs turning in her sister's head—she was already planning her next TikTok, already trying to figure out how she could twist this to make herself the victim.

The judge wasn't finished.

"You have been found guilty of defamation. You will remove all defamatory content. You will cease all commentary on Mrs. Morgan and Mr. Morgan. You will pay damages, including full reimbursement for their legal fees." He paused. "Though, given your financial situation, I suspect that last one will remain unpaid."

Lina exhaled slowly. There it was. The victory. The validation. Michelle had lost. Funny how, removed from the oversight of their father, everyone saw Michelle for exactly what she was.

The moment they stepped out of the courthouse, Lina felt the weight lift from her shoulders. She stood still for a long moment, eyes closed, the crisp autumn air filling her lungs.

Sam stood beside her, silent, but she could feel his presence like a shield—solid, unwavering.

She turned to him. "You're going to respond to him now, aren't you?"

Sam smiled, slow and sharp. "Oh, absolutely." He pulled out his phone, scrolled to Arlo's text from months ago, and finally—finally—typed his response.

Arlo, you have spent Lina's entire life treating her like she is worthless, and now, you will never know the person she has become. And that is your loss. Not hers. You have lost your daughter. You will never know the kindness and brilliance and resilience that she carries. You will never know how deeply she is loved by those who actually deserve her.

He paused, rereading his words before adding one final line.

I look forward to never hearing from you again, and so does she.

He hit send.

Lina let out a slow breath.

Then, without another word, she reached for his hand. And together, they walked away.

Big Enough So You Can't Hurt Her
Three Years Later

The morning light stretched long and golden over the rolling fields, spilling like honey over the dew-kissed grass. The air was crisp, laced with the scent of damp earth and wildflowers, and carried the distant hum of crickets still lingering from the night. A faint mist curled over the distant hills, rising in slow, languid tendrils as the sun warmed the land.

Lina stood barefoot on the wide porch, a steaming mug of coffee cradled in her hands, watching the world awaken. The acreage she and Sam had bought sprawled before her, lush and endless, their sanctuary carved into the Pennsylvania countryside, far enough from Jim Thorpe to feel like a different lifetime, but close enough that ghosts still whispered in the wind, though they couldn't bother them anymore.

From the barn, the donkeys brayed their morning complaints, their shaggy heads poking over the fence as they waited impatiently for their breakfast. The goats had already climbed onto the wooden beams, bleating indignantly, while the chickens pecked their way through the yard, their feathers ruffled in the cool breeze.

Sam was already outside, moving through the morning chores with the easy rhythm of someone who had long since fallen in love with this life. He scattered grain for the hens, ruffling the head of a particularly bold rooster who had taken a liking to him. The early light caught in his hair, sun-bleached from years in the open air, and Lina let her gaze linger on him, on the strength of the man she had built this world with.

A life she had built without Arlo.

Sophie, stretched luxuriously along the porch railing, flicked her tail as if in agreement, her deep blue eyes fixed on the pastures like she ruled over it all. Now an ancient cat, she had softened into a creature of habit and quiet wisdom, her once sleek body dusted with silver. She was still regal, still untouchable, still the only thing that had loved Lina without conditions from the very start.

Lina took a sip of her coffee, the warmth spreading through her as she watched Sam move through the yard. This was home. This was love. This was peace.

And then the phone rang.

The moment she saw the name, something inside her felt like it curdled. Katrina.

She let the phone ring for a moment before answering, lifting it to her ear with the kind of detachment one reserves for bad news already known.

"Lina," Katrina said, without preamble. "Arlo's dead." The words settled heavily between them, blunt and unmoving.

Lina inhaled slowly, exhaling through her nose as she turned her gaze back to the fields, watching the wind ripple through the tall grass. "How?" she asked, her voice even.

"Heart attack. It was sudden." A pause. "I thought you'd want to know." Katrina said.

There was a long stretch of silence where neither of them spoke.

Lina had imagined this moment a thousand times. What it would feel like.

How it would land inside of her. If there would be a release, if there would be grief, if there would be anything beyond the dull weight of inevitability.

Instead, she only felt... distant.

There was a tinge of sadness. Not for him, but for the idea of him. Arlo had been old, and tired, and empty for as long as she had known him. He had lived his life in the shadow of his own imagined brilliance, convinced of his own superiority even as the world moved on without him. He had been given every opportunity, every chance, and had squandered them all.

And he had never, not once, been a father to her.

His death—the death of the man he truly was, not the man Lina had once wished he could be—did not feel like losing a father. It felt like the closing of a book she had never been a character in, the final sentence of a story she had spent her whole life trying to rewrite. He had been a stranger wearing the title of Dad, a ghost whose presence had been more absence than anything else.

And yet, his absence had still been a wound—one that had never quite healed, one that had ached in the desperate moments when she had let herself hope. Now, even the possibility of closure was gone. There would be no reckoning, no moment of clarity, no father standing in front of her with eyes finally open, seeing her for the first time.

There was just an ending. And a hollow kind of sadness for the man who had never been more than a mirage, slipping through her fingers every time she reached for him.

"I appreciate the call," Lina said finally, her voice unreadable.

Katrina hesitated. "The funeral is on Saturday. Michelle's already making a mess of things."

Lina let out a breath, closing her eyes for a moment. "I won't be there," she said.

Another pause. A sharp exhale. "You sure?" Katrina's voice became sharp, almost scornful. "He was your father, and he was a good man." She said angrily.

"Yes." Lina was sure. This was something she had put to bed a long time ago.

More silence. Then Katrina sighed. "I figured as much. He always said you were a self-involved bitch." With that, the call ended, Katrina offering a perfunctory take care before the line went dead.

Lina stood there for a long moment, the wind moving through the trees, rustling the leaves in a sound like whispered confessions. She had spent years believing that if she let go of Arlo, if she let herself truly move on, she would carry guilt like an anchor. That if he died without her having done everything to fix things, she would regret it for the rest of her life.

But standing here now, in the home she had built, in the life she had carved from the wreckage of his indifference, she felt no regret. Because the truth had always been there, lurking beneath all of her hope.

He had never been capable of loving her.

And now, he never would.

She had lost nothing.

Two weeks later, Katrina's name lit up Lina's phone again, the ringing cutting through the peaceful hum of the late afternoon. Lina leaned against the kitchen counter, her fingers wrapped around a cooling cup of coffee, watching Sam through the wide kitchen window. Outside, the sun stretched golden across the acreage, casting long, honeyed shadows over the pasture. Sam was fixing part of the barn fence, his movements fluid, practiced, his sun-kissed arms flexing as he hammered a new beam into place. A gust of wind stirred the trees at the edge of their land, shaking loose the last of the autumn leaves, sending them tumbling in crisp, coppery spirals to the ground.

Sophie, curled up on the counter beside Lina, let out a small sigh, her tail flicking in lazy disinterest as her phone continued to ring.

Lina didn't want to answer. She had nothing more to say to Katrina. Still, after the fourth ring, she picked up.

Katrina's voice on the other end was frantic, edged with raw desperation. "I need your help."

Lina inhaled slowly, her gaze drifting back to the barn, where she could see that Sam was whistling softly to himself as he worked. The goats had gathered by the fence, watching him like a captivated audience, their ears twitching at every sound. The air smelled of hay and woodsmoke, the scent drifting from the firepit where they had roasted marshmallows the night before.

She turned away from the peaceful scene, stepping deeper into the kitchen. "What's wrong?" she asked, though she already knew, and was already well aware she wanted nothing to do with the situation that would be unfolding.

"It's Michelle," Katrina's voice was tight, shaking. "She's trying to take everything—Arlo's house, his things, the little money he left behind. She's threatening me, trying to throw me out."

Lina remained silent, letting Katrina unravel as she continued.

"She says it all belongs to her," Katrina went on, her words spilling over each other in a rush. "She's screaming at me, calling me a thief, saying I was just some gold-digging bitch who never deserved to be here. She's getting violent, Lina. I don't know what to do."

Lina closed her eyes, tilting her head slightly as she listened. The wind had picked up outside, rattling the chimes that hung on the porch, their hollow, melodic sounds carrying through the open window.

"I need a lawyer," Katrina pleaded. "Your lawyer. You can help me fight her. You have the money, the resources—"

And there it was. The thing her family always seemed to believe about her. That because she had something, she must owe them something.

She didn't rush to answer. Instead, she absorbed it all—the desperation, the tangled mess of consequences Katrina had let herself walk into.

She had known exactly who Michelle was. She had married a man who had let his eldest daughter get away with everything, who had given and given while Michelle had taken and taken, unchecked, unchallenged. And now, Katrina was left in the wreckage, shocked that the storm had finally turned on her. When Katrina finally ran out of words, Lina exhaled softly.

"I'm sorry you're dealing with this," she said gently. "I hope it works out for you." Her voice resonated with the deep disconnect she felt.

Silence.

"...That's it?" Katrina's voice turned sharp, incredulous.

"That's it." Lina replied breathily. Her voice reflecting the lightness she felt inside.

"You're seriously not going to help?" Katrina sounded incensed, her words rising to anger as she posed her question.

"No." Lina confirmed. "It's not my circus, and it's not my monkeys." This was a saying she had always loved. It gave her great pleasure to be saying it now about the family she had never been a part of after her mother passed away.

A bitter laugh crackled through the line. "You're really just going to let Michelle win?"

Lina turned back toward the window, watching the donkeys lazily flicking their tails, the chickens scratching in the dirt, Sam wiping the sweat from his forehead as he straightened from his work. This was her life. The only life that mattered.

"I left that life behind a long time ago," she said simply.

And then, with the kind of finality that left no room for argument, she ended the call.

That evening, as the sun bled into the horizon, streaking the sky in deep oranges and purples, Lina and Sam sat on the porch. The world around them was settling, the animals huddling into their shelters, the crickets beginning their nightly song. Sophie sat perched on the railing, her gaze sharp, watching the last sliver of daylight disappear beyond the trees.

Lina let out a slow breath, her hands wrapped around a mug of peppermint tea, the steam curling into the cool night air.

"She called again," she said, her voice even, steady.

Sam, seated beside her, stretched his legs out, his arm draping over the back of her chair. "Let me guess," he mused. "Michelle's trying to devour whatever's left, and Katrina thinks you should fix it?"

Lina huffed a quiet, detached laugh. "More or less."

Sam turned his head to look at her, his expression unreadable in the dim light. "And what did you say?"

She smiled faintly, running her fingers over the rim of her mug. "I wished her well and hung up."

Sam's slow, pleased chuckle rumbled through the night. "Smart girl. I'm proud of you."

They sat in silence for a moment, the peace of their home wrapping around them like a well-worn blanket. Lina tipped her head back, gazing at the stars above, stretched wide and infinite.

"I don't know why she thought I'd help," she murmured.

Sam took her hand, lacing his fingers through hers. "Because they still think you owe them something."

Lina turned to him, and in the moonlight, she saw the way he was looking at her—with pride, with warmth, with the kind of unwavering love she had spent her whole life searching for. "You don't," he confirmed softly.

She reached out to him and squeezed his hand, nodding. And for the first time, she truly, deeply knew it.

Her father had been broken. He had been incapable of loving her. Incapable of loving anyone beyond the illusion of himself and his eldest daughter that he had constructed. But that was no longer Lina's burden to carry.

The wind moved through the fields, rustling the tall grass, carrying with it the echoes of the past, the remnants of ghosts she no longer needed to chase.

She had survived them. And in the end, that was the greatest victory of all.

She turned to Sam, a slow, easy smile stretching across her lips. "Come on," she said, rising to her feet, her body light, untethered. "Let's go feed the donkeys their dinner."

And with that, she walked toward the life she had built, toward the love she had always deserved, toward the peace she had carved from the wreckage.

Free. Finally, finally free.

You've Reached The End But...
The Stories Never Stop

Songs To Stories is exactly what it sounds like—short, emotionally devastating, romantically charged, and occasionally unhinged novellas inspired by the one and only Taylor Swift. Because why simply listen to a song when you can spiral into an entire fictional universe about it?

A new novella drops on the 13th of every month, so if you have commitment issues, don't worry—you don't have to wait long for your next dose of heartbreak, longing, and characters making wildly questionable life choices in the name of love.

To keep up with the latest releases, visit BrittWolfe.com—or don't, and risk missing out while the rest of us are already crying over the next one. Your call.

See you at the next emotional wreckage.

About The Author
Britt Wolfe

Britt Wolfe was born in Fort McMurray, Alberta, and now lives in Calgary, where she battles snow, writes stories, and cries over Taylor Swift lyrics like the proud elder Swiftie she is. She loves being part of a fan base that's as passionate as it is melodramatic.

She's married to a smoking hot Australian (her words, but also probably everyone else's), and together they parent two fur-babies: Sophie, the most perfect husky in the universe, and Lena, a mischievous cat who keeps them on their toes—and their furniture in shreds.

When Britt's not writing or re-listening to "All Too Well (10 Minute Version)," she's indulging her love for reading, potatoes in all forms, and the colour green. She's also a huge fan of polar bears, tigers, red pandas, otters, Nile crocodiles, and—because they're underrated—donkeys.

Her life is full of love, laughter, and just enough chaos to keep things interesting.

 @the.banality.of.britt

 BrittWolfe.com